LOST &
FOUND

. . . LOST

LOST &

FOUND

text by Judith Thurman

pictures by Reina Rubel

ATHENEUM · NEW YORK · 1978

. . . FOUND !

LIBRARY OF CONGRESS CATALOGING IN PUBLICATION DATA

Thurman, Judith.   Lost and found.

SUMMARY: Explores in poetry different kinds of losses
and the delights of finding.
[1. American poetry]   I. Rubel, Reina.   II. Title.
PZ8.3.T42Lo   811′.008   77-21037
ISBN 0-689-30611-3

Published simultaneously in Canada by
McClelland & Stewart, Ltd.
Printed in the United States of America by
The Connecticut Printers, Hartford, Connecticut
Bound by The Book Press, Brattleboro, Vermont
First Edition

FOR
Jonathan and George

LOST & FOUND

Who knows
where a lost thing
goes . . .

. . . when the wind
blows?

High tide
licks your feet,
melts
your sand walls—

There they go!

But look!

Low tide
strews
sea jewels
at your feet.

Under
paved streets,
which lie like lids
on junk
the earth has saved,

lost cities
have been found:
old tools and pots,
strange stones;

the ribs and jaws
of dinosaurs . . .

And digging
in the hard ground
of a yard . . .

How many boots,
how many mittens
have you lost?

(Left ones, right ones?)

How many hats?
How many buttons—

(Loose ones, tight ones?)

Do you suppose
they've made
scare-clothes
for the scarecrows?

Sometimes
a puppy
runs away—

He's really lost.

Sometimes
a kitten
is only hiding.

You found him!

Have you lost
a tooth yet?
A new one will sprout
where the old one
fell out . . .

Hair, too,
will grow . . .

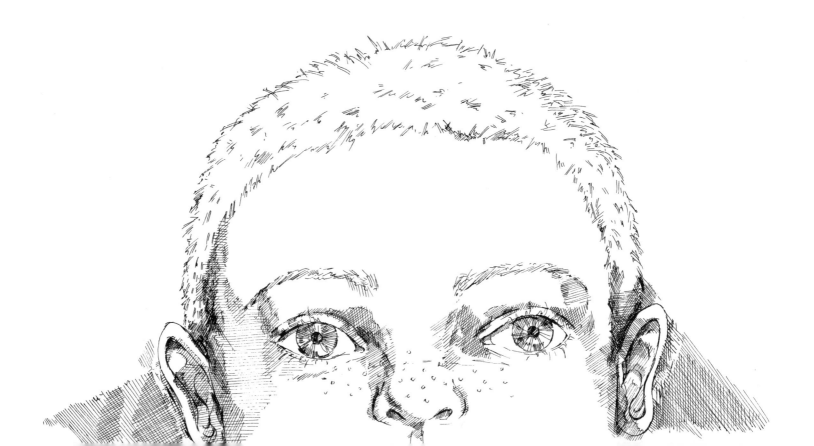

Not always,
though.

A snake
loses
his crisp,
old skin . . .
wriggles out.

A new one
grows in.

The chameleon
loses
herself
before
your eyes—
on every leaf
her coat is
a disguise.

The zebra, too,
slips out of sight,
plays tricks on you
in black and white.

. . . LOST

Someone
can always use
what you lose.

FOUND!

Someplace,
lost toys
dream . . .

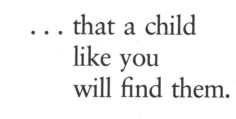

. . . that a child
like you
will find them.

THE END